Riverland
and other Poems

Eileen Bell

Riverland explores a memory from Eileen's childhood on a riverfront property near Kamloops. Other poems explore her relationship with the landscape and memories of Kamloops. Yet others wander farther afield. Her encaustic art accompanies the poetry showing landscapes and other visions.

Riverland and other Poems
Eileen Bell

Copyright 2017
Second Edition Copyright 2020

Feasgar by Joan Coldwell
Where I am From by Natasha Ablack
Acrylic Paintings from Rachel Anderson
Used by permission of authors.

Original Artwork by Eileen Bell

ISBN 978-1-989092-29-3

RIVERLAND

Restless River winds
winnowing valley farmland.

In Father's garden hens squawk.
Silver sunlight dances.

Hens prance single file.
Fowl feet indent narrow path.
Spurn garden's bounty
for girl in dusty pants
rattling evenings grain bowl.

Wind rustles treetops.

Rachel Anderson

FEASGAR

The dusk burdened with our dreams lies still.
A silver shroud enfolds both land and sea.
These gracious moments of eternity
the waning days with haunted beauty fill.
This is ours, this hallowed place of dreams,
steeped in deep peace and fraught with strange allure,
like wind bourne music, a vagrant silver strain;
when all the world is tired and no star gleams.
Here as of old we find despair to cure.
Pine scented darkness and the healing rain.

Joan Coldwell/1932/Scotland

Feasgar translates from Scottish Gaelic to the English word 'twilight'

HEIRLOOMS

Don't try on the shame clothes from the heirloom closet.
Put them back on the hangers.
They smell musty with despair.
Tracing time-lines of decay;
back to the infancy of meagreness.
Grandmother's steamer trunk
bearing tattling travel stickers
Gresford, to Halifax
Across Canada by train,
to end her journey west.

Grandmother:
Longing for well-kept tales of her homeland,
 later returned to Wales.

Truculent trunk, forgotten in the corner of childhood's closet,
Wary of soft-eyed girls with grubby poking fingers
My friend and I, one summer afternoon,
eager for clues, lift cranky hinges.
Dusty secrets from her worried wardrobe.
Crabby closet of yesterday's creations, a fox-fur collar, rancorous
with neglect, startled from its sleeping slink.
Beady eyes and snapping jaw
sees us leaning into his fusty world.
In our flurried imaginations
snaps at our small faces.

The lid bangs shut.
Later we peek inside:
to find a perfectly fitting bra
transforming my friend
embracing embarrassments grown -up gift
of not having to ask mother for a first bra.

Dancing about in girlish eagerness,
we spot a brightly painted ceramic hen, eager for new life
broody in the box.
I pick it up too quickly
hand slips on the raised surface
hen smashes into pieces.
"Busted."
"Close the lid."
"Quick, throw the bra back too."
"Hide it from mother, she never looks in here."

This missive for life rattles round in my head.
Childhood survival and later - habit.
'Close the lid carefully now.'
'No one will know.'
Kept secrets from husband, children and friends,
no one will ever look inside
to see how crammed a wardrobe of shame clothes hangs in
heirloom's closet.
Now age overtakes:
Time to open the door and snoop again.
How to look inside without trying on grandma's bra or smashing
ceramic chickens?
Don't put on the shame clothes.

The fox-fur collar once beady eyed and snapping
lies lifeless, moth -eaten and covered in dust on the closet floor.
Weep with your children for what can never be; for what is
forever lost.

Open the windows.
Air out the closet.
Pack up the past.

Dance in the street.

ROCKING CHAIR

I am a rocking chair,
made from human flesh and hair.
I have a smile and hands to hold
a book of stories yet untold,
of dogs that know of human speech,
of dusty rooms where old men sleep.
Where children dance past time and space
and rainbows color sunshine's face.

Clocks to track your hearts soft rhyme
not of use for story-time.
Grow wings and flutter over sill
then return to doorway-still
and listen with enchanted pale,
as wings brush breath of summer's tale.
Soft as waiting breeze exhales
such wonder as my tales enthrall
past tick of time to bend and fall
to rock the world of greed and rush
to gentle sway of stories hush.

TALISMAN

My child; I dreamed
You and I walked the streets
of a strange unearthly city.
Surprised, when welcomed to tea
in a hotel room on the Fourth floor.

A talisman
inhabiting that radiant dimension
served an elixir
of compassion for our suffering
even of which we did not speak.

He said: Pain is only an element of existence
over whose creation one has no power
Flashing daggers of hate and anger
to ward off earthly torments
your weapons only bend and warp
as a child's toy left too long in the sun.
Nature continues to create
the hand that turns the knife into the heart of the child
and the drop of dew on the rose petal.

In dreams pure perfection
fortuitous fortune
in the form of a small earthly man
make me conscious that reason and love agree;
You and I are not guilty of suffering.

Now as I watch you,
Twisting in pain on the floor,
I recoil from natures indifference,
then realize: Reason and Love agree.
Love exists across time and space
You and I are not guilty of suffering.

TOMBSTONES

Charlotte Bronte never suspected
the innocent act of hanging sheets to dry
over tombstones outside the parsonage
could be spreading tuberculosis bacilli
to her family and villagers of Haworth.

The women of Haworth grumbled
at the Curate's disallowing sheets to dry over
tombstones.
 "Never saw the like and what's it his business?"
"A man telling us how to do our washing
and a Curate at that."

Was this a simple man's glimpse
into an understanding about the spread of disease?
Sewage flowed through the streets.
Water pumped for household use; unfit for
consumption unwittingly breeds consumption.

Inside the parsonage the lonely motherless girls and
their brother Branwell
inspired each other,
won great battles, wrote stories,
acted them out.
Plays of love overcoming impossible odds.

One by one they all wasted away.
The two oldest sisters small tubercular bodies
buried in the parsonage graveyard
leaking bacteria into the ground.
Underground tunnels of rats and disease
crept into their home.

Charlotte, Emily and Anne's stories
earlier bred from the unchecked exuberance of
childhood
later delighted fashionable London Society.
The unchecked battle in the graveyard and laneways of
Haworth
needed a true champion.

Lonely tombstones trembled under furious night
winds shucking off suspect sheets.
Standing stones, like frail knowing old friends
in their crumbled dignity
unable to speak of the horrors seeping underneath
which bled into welcoming pools of street sewage
making easy prey of the frail and undernourished.

Today we delight in the novels of these brave, young women.
Their childhood heroes such as the 'Duke of Wellington' and 'Napoleon'
never fought the battle of having to convince the women of Haworth
to remove their sheets from the parsonage and graveyard tombstones.

Rachel Anderson

NOLITE TRADERE

Royal is our Race.
McGregor.
Never held the Scottish throne.
The race to Royal is the telling
of a true King or Queen.
Ancestors hold spell over us yet.
Generations and an ocean removed.
Rob Roy
dances still over the highlands,
defending kin with sword.
Fierce honour
and trusted word.
Robert the Bruce
never defeated
weeps and schemes still
in his spider lair.
'Nolite Tradere'.
Bell, united with McGregor
carry the motto,
Royal is our Race.
Canadian descendants
after years of patient telling
relive later heroes.
Masters of pen and pulpit

Harbingers of democracy
cultivating ideas of honour, beauty and independence,
long before we decided
freedom was invented in America.
Science and its usefulness,
produced engineers.
The London underground proudly echoes
calculations of our lineal uncle.
What the earliest defenders of the common man
already knew
the advocate guilds put into words.
The dictates of reason mean more that the law itself.
Royal is our Race.
Neither weakened by time or place.
Abundant in our children's markings
Shrieking gannets, sea- sky
rocky cliffs
hold spell over us yet.
Mother's crooning holds me fast
to a small boat across a chill ocean.
Flora MacDonald
Hastening the bonny prince
to a stopover on the Isle of Skye.

HAIKU

Haiku is as poetry
a feeling unnamed
a world minus I or we.

A breathless undercurrent creeps
as a root through a cracked cellar wall
Stealth wind whispers
inside a warm afternoon rain.

To What Remains

Poetry doesn't come with instructions
Neither do men.
both beg to have mysteries unlocked
they like to make their work challenging
the best methods are scattered
among recipes tossed carelessly over mind's sagging shelf
With men I try to measure word ingredients carefully
a right amount of nutmeg blended into the eggs, butter and cheese
savoury and dill
a little cayenne for a thrill
hoping to bring out the flavours deep from within his heart.

Later I sigh
souffle sits on counter
tipsy -pan man
crooked smirk of consolation
I smash my fingers through the center of his leering egginess.

I piece it together and serve
eating together not quite ordinary
eggs cheese and bacon go down easy
We toast a little sweet red

'To What Remains.'

Gertrude Stein sits across my kitchen table
only a single sheeted poem separates us
how do I dissolve deceptive witty bites of words
designed to keep us apart.

I picture the puffy souffle, recently baked
a toothpick in the middle
sizzle-pop
her poem still remarkable
delicious with a little fruit.

"All the goods are stolen; all the blisters are in the cup."
(Gertrude Stein-quote)
relationships based on false assumptions?
blights passed back and forth unknowingly
with a sweet sip from your wine cup
destroying happiness from inside.

Gertrude smiles enigmatically
wordlessly direct
passes me a glass of port
we toast silently, then sip.

'To What Remains.'

Teen Spirit

What does "Smells Like Teen Spirit" mean.
What does it smell like-
Deodorant?
I sit alone on the couch at night
Talking to myself.
Shadows from street lights
Cast an eerie light over the living room.

I muse over this song title
While my teenagers are out
partying --

What does it mean?

I never ask my girls how they see it.
I need something to do while they are out.
Maybe Kurt Cobain is a genius.

Did he know mums like me would sit alone
muttering incoherently over the words
"Smell Like Teen Spirit"
while their 16 year olds are
OUT

doing all the things they had been carefully
taught not to do?

If I could figure out the real meaning
Would they stay home?

Angst--
Is this just for teenagers?
I sigh wearily on my way to bed
and leave the front door unlocked.

In my Bed of Dreams

I lie in my bed of dreams
Suffused
In drowsy blankets.
Somewhere in your head or mine
A scream of pain renders me conscious.

Through the open window
The moon – insistent
The dark sky beyond.

The moon is my soul's light
My vision of you
Behind your barred window
Choking on the wretchedness
Of not being heard.

"Take everything away except the bed
In case she hurts herself."

How far have we come from the 'Yellow Wallpaper'
Cure?
Does Charlotte Gillman rest easy now?

The security guard poised by the door
Gun ready
To attack the violence of emptiness.

Better a Faith Healer or a Nun in a funny hat
To watch over
The futile ferocity of the mentally ill.

Beyond the bars
The silent specter gleams
Between a million misspent stars
You, beside a crackling campfire
and your little girl
with hopeful brown eyes
that dance in the portent light.

Old Roads

Before:

Kamloops was a place I wanted to get away from.
Scratchy sagebrush
Barren hills
Apple orchards and river-land
Disappearing into sixties subdivisions.

What good was this place?
Treeless wasteland--
Dirt roads leading nowhere--
hard to nurture any living thing.
I was withering at seventeen.
Heart dry and bitter
from yearning to be free.

Lately:

I stand in a clearing at Monte Creek
Once there were ranches, graceful homes, tennis courts, a general store.
An unpainted wooden Church still stands atop a hill.
I feel at one with this bristly brushland.
A kinship with what will never be again.

I search:

long the highway for the "Welcome to Monte Creek"
sign.
It stood as a lonely beacon to history after the area was
deserted.
Swallowed by the earth— adorning someones living
room?

Russian Olives festoon this highway.
Restless renegades
sweep sweetly
as brooms along the brush-way
remembering--
whispering--
one branch bent towards the next.
Mis-heard stories
as in a child's game.
What emerges may be a different story.
I long for the secrets in the swish of wind
telegraphing between the trees.

No subdivisions here.

I am Haunted:

by recollections of dirt roads
East of Clearwater.
sunny summer days
No end in sight.
Dust between my toes
Sheep in summer pastures
a cold creek
a stick to poke rocks
a cabin with a soft chair and a book along the way.

Today:

Driving along Tranquille Road
crowded behind
a rickety wooden fence
a front yard giddy with apple trees
budding pink against the Spring wind.

In the Fifties:

Mr. Desmond drove a horse-driven milk cart
around Brocklehurst.
Horses left more deposits on our dirt road
than dimes given for a quart of milk.

In the Fifties:

rag-tag kids- dawdlers
wishing for candy or orange pop
discover prize-worthy nickels or dimes
along gravel roadway.
Hands push found money
across tall counter
jowls pouched with candy.
Sticky glass bottles clutched proudly in small, dirty
hands.

I Miss:

"Town and Country Store"
with the mewing cat no-one minded
sniffing out the groceries
across the high counter
black greasy candies
jaw- breakers, two for a nickel.

After the Store:

Laughing through black candy lips.
traipsing home across the cow pasture
our tongues sweet-licorice
against the salt-licks.

Now:

Tim Horton's beckons us
with its comforting sameness
standing where country store once stood.
No dimes for a double-double.

Salvaged Memories:

Redemption.
From a dusty village to an energetic city.
It rains more often these days
on the clay soil of my childhood.

Painted Horse Road

Mottled skirmish of cloud
Streaks of sunshine above mountain prairie,
lingering over neighbour' farms.
Dogs wag tails; nip each other
along the county road you named.
'Painted Horse Road.'

Neighbours serve tea and empathy.
The coldness and anger of my world
melt away when I step past your doorway.

Blue wax wash of mountains
etches across the Montana sky.

Friendship unfolds over a table of paint
colours quick from the box
impatient to dazzle.
I discover in a swirling haste of colour
flowers larger than life.
Angels hover above.
Wide eyed fish stare from a frozen river.

You plan and hold tight to brush
meticulously painted flowers
birds ready to fly off the paper.
I am splattered with paint.
You sit in quiet concentration.

Realists find reason to stay home.
Close knit through the years.
Laughing faces around the Christmas tree.
From your kitchen window
steaming horses- snorting at hay bales
forked over the paddock.
Biting winter air.

Autumns bonfires bring out the grandchildren.
Strong limbed boys stacking the fire.
Love's forty acres
holding close across the years.

Dreamers seek their way
in pursuit of clearer paths.

In this tiny apartment.
I stare at the meadowlark you painted
worrying among the rocks and roots.

I think of stretching farm fields
the scratchy, summer smell of wheat
Dogs whipping wrens across stubble-fields.

On a cold winter morning in Canada.

Creation

Pressing against the window,
watching a storm.
A crack of thunder.
Forks of lightening crackle
serving up a devilish dish of danger.
Downed power lines, broken trees.
A small girl behind a thin pane of glass.

Emerging from the mist, I see God shivering beside a tree.
Cloak is soaked; Water in his sandals.
Shaking his staff: Thundering at the sky like Moses.
"Do you not heed my commands. You have gone too far this time."
His voice echoes over the river and mountains.
Then another crash of thunder.
God or Jesus?
I wondered.
I imagine he was wonderfully scared; a little happy like me.
Not a good place for God.
Better with me; behind the glass.

Mother's benign neglect favours me.
Free to stand against the window; free to take on risk.
Free to place a sodden Deity
in a hollow beside a tree in the back yard.

Mother is busy consoling my terrified brother
gasping tears under the table
his hands pressed over ears.

One night in a storm
God may die by his own creation.
Then who will make thunder grumble against the heavens?
Who will flash lightening past my window
and design the pattering of soft rain on the rooftop,
lulling me to sleep.

How will I know he is gone?
Only in the stillness of the ghostly morning.
Is he lurking behind the fog?
Watching...

My rubber boots squeak along the path.
A crow squawks.
Grasshoppers show tiny, resilient faces.
Bodies,
teetering on waves of sparkling grass.

I stare at mud -filled hollow under God's tree.
Drowned or swallowed under?

A patch of blue sky; A little breeze
I am skipping past the wind.

For My Mothers

A Prayer for peace and clarity. Gratitude for the presence of wellness and vitality.

Virtuous, standing at the edge of her crumbling earth. Behind lays the paths she has walked.

Stepping heavy has caused the mantle and rock to crack, pouring unfathomable sensations, taunting a molten core, to a surface floor.

Eroding all that remains. If she stays still she will drop to the waves, to the sea and become part of the infant island soil.

Trusting in the unknown depths of the ocean, she steps off the edge of all she has ever known. To plant her brave toes, stepping stones form under her foot. Treading lightly, she must leave her imprint thoughtfully for she is the first one to mark these new lands. Ought to be making every action count. Taking one step at a time, off the edge of all she has ever known.

Towards the sun rising, beyond frontiers of familiarity. Courage curls to deepen the breath, unfurling life welcomed to grow in this home.

If she had been washed into the sea she would have not been able to walk this untouched paradise, a habitat to reflect a pure heart of compassion, clear and silent mind.

    Natasha Ablack.

Without Me

I fell in love with you
for a week in 2012.
We met in a small cafe
as friends from the seventies.

I recall an eager, awkward boy.
Not so when we met again..
Tall and blond as ever
but with a new aspect.
You had become a writer
an actor in TV commercials
a Mall- Santa..

You tell me you had been in love.
I remember when you asked me to marry you
on the summer steps of my first house.
I was married, mother of a baby girl.

In 1972
I didn't understand steadiness and kindness.
I only knew impulsiveness and ambivalence.
You were in love.
I was mildly curious.

In the small cafe in 2012, I fall in love.
You take me through your years of struggle.
I tumble back to mine
smiling at my missed chance at love
sitting across the table.

I see a new honesty in you.
A man who knows himself.
You have a girlfriend.
Been with her for ten years.
She is your rock—you say.
I hide my despair
behind my smile.

We part
promising to keep in touch.
I walk around my apartment
spinning in a web of memories
sequencing the years
whirling through my head.
Then self-doubt
drops me like a concrete boot.

How did I miss the cues?
You were in love.
I was experimenting.
Then I recall the chaos of that decade.
How could we have been other than we were?
Messed up kids.
This is 2012 not 1972.
No more Acid rock and Be-ins
parties where you and I sit
in the corner, slouched against the wall
talking philosophy, laughing absurdly
while others solve the world's problems
with the help of cheap wine and an abundance of pot.

We had an argument in 1971.
I was depressed about my lack of faith
in myself, in my ability to write.
You said, "Just be yourself, It will come."
I said "Lot of good that does for you - being yourself."
"You are the odd-man out."

You call on my 69th birthday.
We make a joke about the seventies coming again
in another incarnation.
Later; I see you on a TV commercial for Nissan.

Yours was the sad albino face in the corner of the screen
yearning still for a beautiful girl
who decorates a sporty car.
Do you ever look back and wonder
What could have been
With Me?

I now admire your courage in facing life.
The awkward boy who yearns to fit in.
A stumbling shadow on a set-less stage
transforming into
the actor who discovers
myriad chances to re-play the odd- man out.
A fascination with ironies also begets
a Santa who speaks truth to troubled kids.

There's a slight limp in your lower, left leg.
that speaks of lonely times.
I love who you have become
because of your struggle through
many indifferent years
without me.

Review by Rita Joan Dozlaw, - Kamloops Columnist

The Heron on the cover called to me from the coffee table top. Who can resist picking up a little book of poems? I'm glad I picked this one up; for, the visions in its stanzas and verses took me on an intriguing sentimental path.

Exquisite encaustic artwork illustrated the pieces enhancing reflections on the past. It was a toss-up as to my favorites. And then, like a finale, the back cover collage of the book's mysterious illustrations melded into a colourfully poetic mosaic.

Cover to cover, my imagination was whetted for a re-read.

Rita Joan Dozlaw

Riverland and Other Poems by Eileen Bell, is a fascinating book of poetry and original artwork by four generations of creative women in her family.

I was captivated by the dreamlike landscapes in the artwork and the strong imagery in these poems lingered long after I read them.

This book is a treat from cover to cover.

Carol Bratvold

Eileen lives in Kamloops, B.C., by the North Thompson River where she enjoys walking the dog. She has a messy garden in the backyard in which she putters about happily.

Contact Eileen through Celticfrog Publishing at celticfrog@live.com

Other Published Works by Eileen Bell
Children's Books
Dog-Gone- 1992,1998
The Keeper of the Shell- 2019- Celtic Frog Publishing
Available on Amazon in hard copy or e-book
Soft cover available from Ingram Spark Publishing
Works in Anthology's
Short Stories- Polar Expressions Publishing- 2015-16
Poetry- Polar Expressions Publishing- 2013- 2016
Poetry Books
Eileen Bell and Friends- Overland Press-2017
River-land and other Poems- Celtic Frog Publishing-2020
Available on Amazon
Eileen Bell is a regular contributor of stories and poems to the New Author's Journal- Mario Farina-Publisher-Quarterly Journal
Available on Amazon in hard copy or e-book.
For other soon to be published works please refer to CelticFrogPublishing.com/Eileen-Bell.

www.ingramcontent.com/pod-product-compliance
Lightning Source LLC
Chambersburg PA
CBHW061212070526
44583CB00025B/3219